Pebble®

Character Values

I Am
Friendly

by Sarah L. Schuette

Consulting Editor: Gail Saunders-Smith, PhD

Consultant: Madonna Murphy, PhD
Professor of Education, University of St. Francis, Joliet, Illinois
Author, *Character Education in America's Blue Ribbon Schools*

Capstone
press®
Mankato, Minnesota

Pebble Books are published by Capstone Press,
P.O. Box 669, 151 Good Counsel Drive, Mankato, Minnesota 56002.
www.capstonepress.com

1 2 3 4 5 6 11 10 09 08 07 06

Library of Congress Cataloging-in-Publication Data
Schuette, Sarah L., 1976–
    I am friendly / by Sarah L. Schuette.
    p. cm.—(Character values)
    Summary: "Simple text and photographs show different ways of being
friendly"—Provided by publisher.
    Includes bibliographical references and index.
    ISBN-13: 978-0-7368-6336-0 (hardcover)
    ISBN-10: 0-7368-6336-2 (hardcover)
    1. Friendship—Juvenile literature. 2. Character—Juvenile literature. I. Title.
II. Series.
BJ1533.F8S33 2007
177'.62—dc22   2006000512

Note to Parents and Teachers

The Character Values set supports national social studies standards for units on individual development and identity. This book describes friendliness and illustrates ways students can be friendly. The photographs support early readers in understanding the text. The repetition of words and phrases helps early readers learn new words. This book also introduces early readers to subject-specific vocabulary words, which are defined in the Glossary. Early readers may need assistance to read some words and to use the Table of Contents, Glossary, Read More, Internet Sites, and Index sections of the book.

Table of Contents

Friendliness

I am friendly.

I am kind

to other people.

I get along with
other people.
I help them when I can.

At School

I play with
a new student at recess.
I help him feel welcome.

I remember
my friend's birthday.
I give him a card.

I smile and say hello to my bus driver.

In the Community

I wave to my neighbor.
I ask her about her day.

I listen to my friend.
I try to cheer her up.

I visit with my friend
who has a broken leg.
I bring him cookies.

Being Friendly

I welcome others
and treat them
with kindness.
It feels good
to be friendly.

Glossary

cheer—to make someone feel good

kind—to be friendly and helpful

recess—a break to rest and play; children have recess at school.

visit—to go see someone and talk with them

welcome—to feel that you belong or fit in a group; people can make other people feel welcome by including them in activities.

Read More

Nettleton, Pamela Hill. *Want to Play?: Kids Talk About Friendliness.* Kids Talk. Minneapolis: Picture Window Books, 2005.

Thoennes Keller, Kristin. *Friendliness.* Everyday Character Education. Mankato, Minn.: Capstone Press, 2005.

Internet Sites

FactHound offers a safe, fun way to find Internet sites related to this book. All of the sites on FactHound have been researched by our staff.

Here's how:

1. Visit *www.facthound.com*

2. Choose your grade level.

3. Type in this book ID **0736863362** for age-appropriate sites. You may also browse subjects by clicking on letters, or by clicking on pictures and words.

4. Click on the **Fetch It** button.

FactHound will fetch the best sites for you!

Index

Word Count: 103
Early-Intervention Level: 12

Editorial Credits
Amber Bannerman, editor; Jennifer Bergstrom, set designer and illustrator;
  Ted Williams, book designer

Photo Credits
Capstone Press/Karon Dubke, all

The author dedicates this book to her school bus driver, Joe Bertrang of Henderson,
  Minnesota. Joe appears on page 12.